Praying Against Marriage Attacks

PRAYING AGAINST MARRIAGE ATTACKS

UNDERSTANDING THE NATURE OF MARRIAGE ATTACKS

HART STEWART

Copyright © 2024 by HART STEWART

Praying Against Marriage Attacks

TABLE OF CONTENT

Praying Against Marriage Attacks

Praying Against Marriage Attacks

INTRODUCTION

Marriage, often described as a sacred union between two individuals, is not immune to the trials and tribulations of life. While many couples embark on this journey with hopes of lifelong happiness and fulfillment, they may find themselves facing unexpected challenges that threaten the very foundation of their relationship. These challenges, commonly known as marriage attacks, can manifest in various forms, including communication breakdowns, financial struggles, infidelity, and external pressures.

In the face of such adversities, the power of prayer emerges as a formidable weapon for couples seeking to safeguard their marriage against attacks. Prayer, deeply rooted in spiritual warfare, provides a channel for divine intervention, strength, and guidance in navigating the storms that may assail the marital bond.

This guide delves into the realm of prayers against marriage attacks, offering insights, strategies, and biblical foundations to empower couples in their spiritual journey together. Through understanding the nature of marriage attacks, harnessing the wisdom of scripture, and employing targeted prayers, couples can fortify their union, cultivate resilience, and emerge victorious over the forces that seek to undermine their love and commitment.

CHAPTER 1

Definition of Marriage Attacks

Marriage attacks encompass a broad spectrum of challenges, adversities, and conflicts that threaten the well-being, stability, and harmony of marital relationships. These attacks can take various forms, ranging from external influences such as societal pressures, financial strains, and career demands, to internal struggles like communication breakdowns, emotional distance, and unresolved conflicts between partners. Marriage attacks may also manifest as infidelity, addiction, or other destructive behaviors that erode trust and intimacy within the relationship. Essentially, marriage attacks are any forces, whether internal or external, that undermine the sanctity, unity, and longevity of the marital bond. Understanding these attacks is crucial for couples seeking to identify, confront, and overcome them through prayer, communication, and concerted efforts to strengthen their relationship.

IMPORTANCE OF PRAYER IN SPIRITUAL WARFARE

Prayer stands as an indispensable weapon in the arsenal of spiritual warfare, particularly in the context of defending

Praying Against Marriage Attacks

marriages against attacks. Here's why prayer holds such paramount importance:

1.   Spiritual Armor: Just as physical armor protects soldiers in battle, prayer serves as spiritual armor for believers facing spiritual warfare. Through prayer, individuals put on the full armor of God, as described in Ephesians 6:10-18, which includes the belt of truth, the breastplate of righteousness, the shoes of the gospel of peace, the shield of faith, the helmet of salvation, and the sword of the Spirit, which is the word of God.

2.   Access to Divine Power: Prayer is the conduit through which believers tap into the boundless power and resources of the Almighty. By seeking God's intervention through prayer, couples invite His presence, guidance, and protection into their marriage, empowering them to withstand and overcome the assaults of the enemy.

3.   Spiritual Discernment: Through prayer, couples gain clarity, wisdom, and discernment to recognize the subtle tactics and schemes of the adversary. Prayer illuminates hidden truths, exposes deception, and equips believers with spiritual insight to effectively combat the forces of darkness.

4. **Unity and Strength:** Joint prayer fosters unity and solidarity between spouses, reinforcing their commitment to stand together against marriage attacks. As they lift their voices in prayer, couples align their hearts, minds, and spirits, drawing strength from each other and from God to confront adversity as a unified front.

5. **Transformation and Healing:** Prayer is a catalyst for spiritual transformation and healing within marriages. As couples surrender their concerns, fears, and burdens to God in prayer, they experience His transformative power working in their hearts and relationships, bringing restoration, healing, and renewal.

6. **Persistent Warfare:** Spiritual warfare is not a one-time battle but a continuous struggle against the forces of darkness. Prayer provides a means for ongoing communication with God, enabling couples to engage in persistent warfare, remaining vigilant and steadfast in their defense against marriage attacks.

In essence, prayer is not merely a passive plea for divine assistance but an active, dynamic engagement in spiritual warfare, empowering couples to confront, overcome, and emerge victorious over the challenges that threaten their marriage.

Praying Against Marriage Attacks

CHAPTER 2
UNDERSTANDING MARRIAGE ATTACKS

"Marriage attacks" typically refer to various challenges or threats that can arise within a marriage or intimate partnership. These challenges can come from internal or external sources and can vary widely in nature. Here are some common types of marriage attacks:

TYPES OF MARRIAGE ATTACKS

Marriage attacks can manifest in various forms, causing stress, strain, and conflict within the relationship. Here are some common types of marriage attacks:

1. **Communication Breakdown:** Poor communication is one of the most common issues in marriages. This can involve misunderstandings, ineffective communication styles, or simply not making time to communicate with each other.

2. **Infidelity:** Extramarital affairs or emotional infidelity can severely strain a marriage. Trust is often broken, and rebuilding it can be a long and difficult process.

3. **Financial Stress:** Money problems, such as debt, overspending, or disagreements about financial priorities, can lead to significant tension in a marriage. Financial stress is one of the leading causes of divorce.

4. **Conflict Resolution Difficulties:** Every couple experiences conflicts, but how they handle them can make or break the relationship. The inability to resolve conflicts healthily and constructively can lead to resentment and distance between partners.

5. **Mismatched Expectations:** Differences in expectations regarding roles, responsibilities, intimacy, or other aspects of the relationship can create friction and dissatisfaction.

6. **External Stressors:** External factors such as job loss, illness, family issues, or societal pressures can put a strain on a marriage and test the resilience of the relationship.

7. **Lack of Intimacy:** Physical or emotional intimacy is crucial for a healthy marriage. When couples drift apart or experience a lack of connection, it can lead to feelings of loneliness and dissatisfaction.

8. **Addiction:** Substance abuse or other forms of addiction can have devastating effects on a marriage, leading to trust issues, financial strain, and emotional turmoil.

9. **Cultural or Religious Differences:** Couples from different cultural or religious backgrounds may face unique challenges in navigating their differences and finding common ground.

10. **Parenting Conflicts:** Disagreements about parenting styles, discipline, or decisions related to children can create tension and conflict in a marriage.

11. **Emotional Neglect:** Ignoring each other's emotional needs, failing to provide support, or withdrawing affection can lead to feelings of loneliness and dissatisfaction in the relationship.

12. **Power Struggles:** Constant conflicts over decision-making, control, or dominance can erode the partnership, leaving one or both partners feeling disempowered or resentful.

13. **Intimacy Issues:** Physical or emotional intimacy may decline due to various reasons, including stress, health issues, or unresolved conflicts, leading to feelings of distance and dissatisfaction.

14. **Parenting Conflicts:** Differences in parenting styles, discipline approaches, or decisions about children's upbringing can cause friction and strain the marriage.

15. **Cultural or Religious Differences:** Differing cultural backgrounds or religious beliefs may create tension and conflict, particularly when it comes to important life decisions and values.

16. **Emotional or Verbal Abuse:** Patterns of emotional manipulation, verbal aggression, or controlling behavior can cause significant harm and distress to the victimized partner, damaging the marriage irreparably.

17. **Sexual Dissatisfaction:** Mismatched libidos, sexual dysfunction, or unresolved sexual issues can

lead to frustration, resentment, and decreased marital satisfaction.

Each of these marriage attacks requires attention, understanding, and proactive efforts from both partners to address and resolve. Seeking couples therapy or counseling can be beneficial in navigating these challenges and rebuilding a strong, healthy marriage.

Couples need to recognize and address these challenges proactively, whether through open communication, seeking therapy, or finding other forms of support. Building a strong foundation of trust, respect, and mutual understanding is key to overcoming marriage attacks and maintaining a healthy and fulfilling relationship.

CAUSES OF MARRIAGE ATTACKS

Marriage attacks, or challenges within a marriage, can stem from a variety of underlying causes. Understanding these causes is crucial for addressing and resolving issues within the relationship. Here are some common causes of marriage attacks:

1.   **Poor Communication:**   Ineffective communication or lack of communication can lead to misunderstandings, unmet needs, and unresolved

conflicts, creating tension and distance between partners.

2. **Unresolved Conflicts:** Failure to address and resolve conflicts can result in ongoing resentment, bitterness, and a breakdown of trust within the marriage.

3. **Lack of Trust:** Trust issues may arise due to past betrayals, secrets, or dishonesty, undermining the foundation of the marriage and causing insecurity and suspicion between partners.

4. **Infidelity:** Extramarital affairs or emotional betrayal can severely damage the trust and intimacy in a marriage, leading to feelings of betrayal, hurt, and anger.

5. **Financial Problems:** Money-related stressors, such as debt, financial instability, or disagreements over spending and saving, can strain the marriage and lead to conflict and resentment.

Praying Against Marriage Attacks

6. **Mismatched Expectations:** Differences in expectations regarding roles, responsibilities, intimacy, or lifestyle can create friction and dissatisfaction within the marriage.

7. **External Stressors:** External factors such as job loss, illness, family issues, or societal pressures can put a strain on the marriage, affecting the emotional well-being and stability of both partners.

8. **Life Transitions:** Major life changes such as becoming parents, relocating, or career shifts can disrupt the dynamics of the marriage and challenge the couple's ability to adapt and support each other.

9. **Emotional Neglect:** Neglecting each other's emotional needs, failing to provide support, or withdrawing affection can lead to feelings of loneliness, resentment, and disconnection within the marriage.

10. **Addiction:** Substance abuse, gambling addiction, or other forms of addictive behavior can strain the marriage, leading to deception, financial instability, and breakdown of trust between partners

11. Cultural or Religious Differences:

Differing cultural backgrounds or religious beliefs may create tension and conflict within the marriage, particularly when it comes to important values, traditions, and decision-making.

12. Unfulfilled Intimacy: Lack of physical or emotional intimacy, sexual dissatisfaction, or unresolved sexual issues can lead to frustration, resentment, and decreased marital satisfaction.

Addressing these underlying causes often requires open and honest communication, empathy, compromise, and sometimes seeking professional help through couples therapy or counseling. Working together to identify and address these issues can strengthen the marriage and improve the overall well-being of both partners.

CHAPTER 3

BIBLICAL FOUNDATIONS FOR PRAYERS AGAINST MARRIAGE ATTACKS

In Christianity, marriage is often regarded as a sacred institution ordained by God, and there are biblical principles and passages that believers may turn to when praying against attacks on marriage. Here are some biblical foundations for prayers against marriage attacks:

1. Genesis 2:24: "Therefore a man shall leave his father and his mother and hold fast to his wife, and they shall become one flesh."

This verse highlights the divine intention for marriage to be a union between one man and one woman, bound together by God.

2. Ephesians 5:25: "Husbands, love your wives, as Christ loved the church and gave himself up for her."

This passage emphasizes sacrificial love within marriage, reflecting the love Christ has for the church. Prayers may seek the strength for husbands to love their wives selflessly and unconditionally.

3. Ephesians 5:22-33: This passage outlines the roles of husbands and wives within marriage, emphasizing mutual submission, respect, and love. Prayers may ask for grace and guidance for both spouses to fulfill their roles according to God's design.

3. 1 Peter 3:7: "Likewise, husbands, live with your wives in an understanding way, showing honor to the woman as the weaker vessel, since they are heirs with you of the grace of life, so that your prayers may not be hindered."

This verse underscores the importance of husbands treating their wives with understanding, respect, and honor, recognizing them as equal partners in God's grace.

4. Matthew 19:6: "So they are no longer two but one flesh. What therefore God has joined together, let not man separate."

This verse emphasizes the sanctity and permanence of marriage, encouraging prayers for protection against anything that may seek to divide or destroy the marital bond.

5. 1 Corinthians 13:4-7: Known as the "love chapter," this passage describes the characteristics of love, including patience, kindness, and perseverance. Prayers may ask for God's help in cultivating these qualities within the marriage relationship.

6. **Philippians 4:6-7:** **"Do not be anxious about anything, but in everything by prayer and supplication with thanksgiving let your requests be made known to God. And the peace of God, which surpasses all understanding, will guard your hearts and your minds in Christ Jesus."**

This passage encourages believers to bring their concerns and anxieties to God in prayer, trusting in His provision, and experiencing His peace.

Prayers against marriage attacks may incorporate these biblical principles, seeking God's protection, guidance, and restoration for the marriage relationship. Believers may also pray for wisdom, discernment, and strength to navigate challenges and uphold the covenant of marriage according to God's will.

SCRIPTURES ON THE SANCTITY OF MARRIAGE

The sanctity of marriage is a central theme throughout the Bible, with numerous scriptures emphasizing the sacredness and importance of this covenant relationship. Here are some key scriptures on the sanctity of marriage:

1. Genesis 2:24: "Therefore a man shall leave his father and his mother and hold fast to his wife, and they shall become one flesh."

This verse from the creation account highlights the divine establishment of marriage as a union between one man and one woman, characterized by unity and permanence.

2. Matthew 19:5-6: "'For this reason, a man will leave his father and mother and be united to his wife, and the two will become one flesh.' So, they are no longer two, but one flesh. Therefore, what God has joined together, let no one separate."

Jesus reaffirms the sanctity and indissolubility of marriage, emphasizing that it is a union established by God Himself.

3. Ephesians 5:31-32: "For this reason, a man will leave his father and mother and be united to his wife, and the two will become one flesh."

This is a profound mystery but I am talking about Christ and the church." In this passage, the apostle Paul connects the marital relationship between husband and wife to the spiritual relationship between Christ and His church, highlighting the sacredness and significance of marriage.

Praying Against Marriage Attacks

4. **Hebrews 13:4:** "Let marriage be held in honor among all, and let the marriage bed be undefiled, for God will judge the sexually immoral and adulterous."

This verse underscores the importance of honoring and preserving the sanctity of marriage, warning against sexual immorality and adultery.

5. **Malachi 2:14-15:** "But you say, 'Why does he not?' Because the Lord was witness between you and the wife of your youth, to whom you have been faithless, though she is your companion and your wife by covenant."

This passage from the Old Testament prophet Malachi emphasizes God's witness to the marriage covenant and the importance of faithfulness and commitment within marriage.

6. **1 Corinthians 7:4:** "The wife does not have authority over her own body but yields it to her husband. In the same way, the husband does not have authority over his own body but yields it to his wife." This verse highlights the mutual self-giving and sacrificial love that should characterize the marital relationship.

These scriptures affirm the sanctity, permanence, and divine origin of marriage, providing guidance and encouragement for couples to honor and uphold their marital covenant according to God's design.

EXAMPLES OF COUPLES OVERCOMING ADVERSITY IN THE BIBLE

The Bible is replete with stories of couples overcoming adversity through faith, perseverance, and reliance on God. Here are some examples:

1.   Abraham and Sarah: Abraham and Sarah faced the adversity of infertility for many years. Despite their old age, God fulfilled His promise to them, and Sarah bore a son, Isaac, demonstrating God's faithfulness and the power of His promises (Genesis 17-21).

2.   Elkanah and Hannah: Hannah struggled with infertility and endured the ridicule of her husband's other wife, Peninnah. However, through fervent prayer and faith, Hannah eventually conceived and gave birth to Samuel, whom she dedicated to the Lord (1 Samuel 1).

3.   Joseph and Mary: Joseph and Mary faced the adversity of social stigma and misunderstanding due to Mary's unexpected pregnancy. Despite this, they remained faithful to God's plan and raised Jesus, the Son of God, fulfilling prophecies and playing a crucial role in Salvation history (Matthew 1-2, Luke 1-2).

Praying Against Marriage Attacks

4.   Ruth and Boaz: Ruth, a Moabite widow, faced the adversity of being a foreigner and a widow in Israel.

Through her faithfulness and hard work, she found favor with Boaz, who became her kinsman-redeemer, and they eventually married, becoming ancestors of King David and, ultimately, Jesus (Ruth 1-4).

5.   Isaac and Rebekah: Isaac and Rebekah faced the challenge of infertility as well. Despite this, Isaac prayed to the Lord, and Rebekah conceived twin sons, Jacob and Esau, who went on to play significant roles in the history of Israel (Genesis 25).

6.   Priscilla and Aquila: Priscilla and Aquila were a married couple who worked alongside the Apostle Paul in spreading the gospel. Despite facing persecution and being forced to move from place to place, they remained steadfast in their faith and served as mentors and supporters of many early Christian leaders (Acts 18, Romans 16:3-5, 1 Corinthians 16:19, 2 Timothy 4:19).

These Biblical examples illustrate how couples, through faith, perseverance, and reliance on God, can overcome various forms of adversity and fulfill their roles in God's plan. They serve as sources of inspiration and encouragement for couples facing challenges in their own lives.

CHAPTER 4

STRATEGIES FOR SPIRITUAL WARFARE IN MARRIAGE

Navigating spiritual warfare within marriage requires a strong foundation of faith, prayer, and mutual support. Here are some strategies for engaging in spiritual warfare in marriage:

1. **Prayer:** Regular, fervent prayer is essential for spiritual warfare in marriage. Couples should pray together for protection, wisdom, and guidance in facing spiritual battles. Praying for each other's spiritual well-being and unity in the face of challenges is also crucial.

2. **Biblical Study and Application:** Studying and applying biblical principles to marriage can strengthen couples' spiritual armor. Regularly reading and meditating on Scripture together can provide guidance, encouragement, and discernment in navigating spiritual warfare.

3. **Spiritual Discernment:** Developing spiritual discernment helps couples recognize and resist

Praying Against Marriage Attacks

spiritual attacks. Being alert to subtle influences, such as temptation, deception, or discord, enables couples to respond with faith and wisdom.

4. Open Communication: Maintaining open and honest communication allows couples to discuss spiritual matters openly, share concerns, and support each other in prayer. Creating a safe space for sharing struggles and seeking counsel strengthens the marital bond and fortifies it against spiritual attacks.

5. Mutual Accountability: Holding each other accountable in spiritual matters fosters growth and resilience in the face of spiritual warfare. Couples can encourage each other to stay faithful to God's Word, pray regularly, and resist temptation.

6. Fellowship with other Believers: Engaging in fellowship with other believers provides support, encouragement, and accountability. Couples can seek guidance from trusted spiritual mentors or participate in couples' Bible studies and prayer groups.

7. Guarding Against Sin: Being vigilant against sin and temptation is crucial in spiritual warfare. Couples should strive to maintain purity in thought, speech, and action, guarding their hearts and minds against influences that may lead them astray.

8. Forgiveness and Reconciliation:

Practicing forgiveness and reconciliation strengthens marital unity and resilience against spiritual attacks. Couples should be quick to forgive each other, seek reconciliation, and extend grace, as modeled by Christ.

9. Resisting Division:

Unity is a powerful defense against spiritual attacks. Couples should guard against division, conflict, and discord, striving to maintain harmony and oneness in their marriage.

10. Seeking Spiritual Guidance:

In times of spiritual warfare, seeking guidance from pastoral counselors, Christian therapists, or spiritual mentors can provide clarity, wisdom, and support in navigating challenges.

By implementing these strategies and relying on God's strength and guidance, couples can effectively engage in spiritual warfare, fortify their marriage, and experience the fullness of God's blessings and protection.

Praying Against Marriage Attacks

CULTIVATING A STRONG SPIRITUAL FOUNDATION AS A COUPLE

Cultivating a strong spiritual foundation as a couple can be a deeply enriching and fulfilling journey. Here are some steps you can take together to strengthen your spiritual bond:

1.   Open Communication: Start by having open and honest conversations about your individual spiritual beliefs, values, and experiences. Share what spirituality means to each of you and how it shapes your lives.

2.   Explore Together: Explore different spiritual traditions, practices, and philosophies as a couple. Attend religious services, meditation classes, or spiritual retreats together. Keep an open mind and be willing to learn from each other's perspectives.

3.   Pray or Meditate Together: Set aside time each day to pray, meditate, or engage in other spiritual practices together. This can help you connect on a deeper level and cultivate a sense of peace and harmony in your relationship.

4.   Reflect and Discuss: Take time to reflect individually and as a couple on your spiritual journey. Discuss how your beliefs and practices are evolving and how they impact your relationship and daily life.

5.   Support Each Other: Be supportive and understanding of each other's spiritual journey, even if you have different beliefs or practices. Encourage each other to grow spiritually and provide emotional support during times of doubt or struggle.

6.   Serve Together: Find opportunities to serve others as a couple, whether through volunteering, charitable giving, or other acts of kindness. Serving others can deepen your sense of connection to something greater than yourselves and strengthen your spiritual bond.

7.   Create Rituals: Establish rituals and traditions that are meaningful to both of you. This could be anything from lighting candles together before dinner to spiritually celebrating special holidays or milestones.

8.   Seek Guidance: If you're facing challenges or seeking deeper insight into your spiritual journey as a couple, consider seeking guidance from a spiritual mentor, counselor, or religious leader who shares your values and beliefs.

Praying Against Marriage Attacks

9. **Practice Gratitude:** Cultivate an attitude of gratitude together by regularly expressing appreciation for each other and the blessings in your lives. Gratitude can help you stay connected and the spiritual dimensions of life.

10. **Stay Connected:** Finally, make time to nurture your relationship and stay connected emotionally, physically, and spiritually. Prioritize quality time together, practice active listening, and continue to support each other's growth and well-being.

By following these steps and being intentional about cultivating your spiritual foundation as a couple, you can deepen your bond, enhance your sense of meaning and purpose, and journey together toward greater spiritual fulfillment.

RECOGNIZING SIGNS OF SPIRITUAL WARFARE IN MARRIAGE

Recognizing signs of spiritual warfare in marriage involves understanding how spiritual forces may impact the relationship dynamics. Here are some signs to be aware of:

1. **Constant Conflict:** If you and your spouse find yourselves frequently arguing over seemingly trivial matters, it could be a sign of spiritual warfare. These conflicts may escalate quickly and seem to have no resolution.

2.   Emotional Distance: Feeling disconnected from your spouse emotionally, even when physically together, may indicate spiritual warfare. It can manifest as a lack of intimacy, emotional support, or understanding between partners.

3.   Negative Thought Patterns: Persistent negative thoughts about your spouse or your marriage, especially those that seem to come out of nowhere or are irrational, might be influenced by spiritual warfare.

4.   Feeling Drained or Oppressed: If you or your spouse experience feelings of fatigue, hopelessness, or oppression without any apparent cause, it could be a sign of spiritual warfare.

5.   Lack of Unity: Difficulty in making decisions together, frequent disagreements on important matters, or a sense of division within the marriage may indicate spiritual warfare at play.

6.   Unexplained Challenges: Facing a series of unexplained challenges or obstacles in your marriage,

Praying Against Marriage Attacks

such as financial struggles, health issues, or relational conflicts, might be a sign of spiritual warfare.

7.   Increased Temptations: Feeling tempted to engage in behaviors that are harmful to the marriage, such as infidelity or substance abuse, can be a sign of spiritual warfare.

8.   Disruption in Spiritual Practices: If you and your spouse experience a sudden disinterest or difficulty in maintaining spiritual practices like prayer, worship, or attending religious services, it could be a sign of spiritual warfare.

9.   Isolation: Feeling isolated from each other or supportive community networks can be a sign of spiritual attack, as spiritual warfare often seeks to divide and conquer.

10.   Intuition and Discernment: Sometimes, a strong intuition or discernment may indicate spiritual warfare. Pay attention to any persistent feelings or insights that suggest something is spiritually amiss in your marriage.

It's important to note that while these signs can indicate spiritual warfare, they can also have other explanations rooted in psychological, emotional, or relational factors.

Seeking guidance from trusted spiritual mentors, counselors, or clergy members can help discern whether spiritual warfare is at play and how to address it effectively. Additionally, cultivating a strong spiritual foundation as a couple through prayer, worship, and mutual support can provide resilience against spiritual attacks.

Praying Against Marriage Attacks

CHAPTER 5

PRACTICAL STEPS TO STRENGTHEN MARRIAGE AGAINST ATTACKS

Strengthening a marriage against attacks involves proactive efforts from both partners to foster communication, trust, and resilience. Here are some practical steps to help strengthen your marriage:

1. **Open Communication:** Encourage open and honest communication between you and your partner. Create a safe space where both of you feel comfortable expressing thoughts, feelings, and concerns without fear of judgment.

2. **Active Listening:** Practice active listening by giving your partner your full attention when they speak. Validate their feelings and show empathy by paraphrasing what they say to ensure understanding.

3. **Quality Time Together:** Make time for each other despite busy schedules. Schedule regular date nights or simply spend quality time together engaging in activities you both enjoy.

4. **Conflict Resolution Skills:** Learn healthy ways to resolve conflicts without resorting to hostility or avoidance. Focus on finding solutions rather than assigning blame.

5. **Building Trust:** Trust is the foundation of a strong marriage. Be honest and reliable in your actions, and follow through on commitments to reinforce trust.

6. **Shared Goals and Values:** Identify common goals and values that are important to both of you. Working towards shared aspirations can strengthen your bond and create a sense of unity.

7. **Support Each Other's Growth:** Encourage personal growth and development in each other. Be supportive of your partner's ambitions and aspirations, and celebrate their successes together.

8. **Maintain Intimacy:** Physical and emotional intimacy are essential components of a healthy marriage. Make time for affection, intimacy, and romance to keep the connection strong.

9. **Manage Stress Together:** Help each other manage stress by providing emotional support and practical assistance when needed. Practice stress-relief techniques together, such as exercise, meditation, or relaxation exercises.

10. Seek Professional Help When Needed:

If you're facing challenges in your marriage that you're unable to resolve on your own, don't hesitate to seek the help of a qualified couple's therapist. Professional guidance can provide valuable insights and strategies for strengthening your relationship.

11. Boundaries and Respect: Establish healthy

boundaries within your marriage and respect each other's individuality. Recognize and honor each other's needs for space, autonomy, and independence.

12. Express Appreciation and Gratitude:

Regularly express appreciation and gratitude towards your partner for the things they do and the qualities you admire in them. Small gestures of kindness and acknowledgment can go a long way in strengthening your bond.

13. Continual Learning: Commit to continually learning about each other and growing together as a couple. Stay curious about your partner's thoughts, feelings, and experiences, and be open to learning new things about them.

By implementing these practical steps and making a conscious effort to prioritize your marriage, you can strengthen your relationship and fortify it against potential attacks. Remember that a strong marriage requires ongoing effort, patience, and commitment from both partners.

PRAYERS AGAINST SPECIFIC MARRIAGE ATTACKS

When facing challenges in marriage, some individuals find comfort in prayer as a way to seek guidance, strength, and protection. Here are some prayers against specific marriage attacks:

PRAYER FOR PROTECTION FROM INFIDELITY:

Heavenly Father, I come before you seeking your protection over my marriage. Guard our hearts and minds against the temptation of infidelity. Help us to remain faithful to one another, honoring the commitment we have made before you. Strengthen the bond of love between us and grant us the wisdom to navigate any challenges that may arise. In your name, I pray, Amen.

PRAYER FOR HEALING FROM PAST HURTS:

Lord, I lift to you the wounds and hurts that have affected my marriage. Heal the pain from past mistakes and transgressions, both mine and my partner's. Help us to forgive one another and move forward with renewed love and understanding. Grant us the grace to let go of resentment and build a future filled with trust and reconciliation. Amen.

PRAYER FOR UNITY IN MARRIAGE:

Gracious God, I pray for unity in my marriage. Help us to be of one mind and spirit, working together as partners in love and harmony. Remove any barriers or divisions that threaten to separate us, and bind us together with cords of compassion and understanding. May our love for one another reflect your love for us, strengthening our bond each day. Amen.

PRAYER AGAINST FINANCIAL STRAIN:

Lord, I bring before you the financial challenges that weigh heavy on my marriage. Provide for our needs and grant us the wisdom to manage our resources wisely. Help us to support one another during times of financial strain, and to lean on you for strength and guidance. Teach us to be good stewards of your blessings and to trust in your provision for our future. Amen.

PRAYER FOR COMMUNICATION AND UNDERSTANDING:

Heavenly Father, I pray for improved communication and understanding in my marriage. Grant us the patience to listen to one another with open hearts and the courage to express ourselves honestly and respectfully. Help us to empathize with each other's perspectives and to find common ground even in times of disagreement. May our communication be a source of strength and unity in our relationship. Amen.

NOTE: Remember that prayer is a deeply personal and individual practice, and these prayers can be adapted or personalized according to your own beliefs, experiences, and specific challenges in your marriage.

PRAYER FOR PROTECTION FROM EXTERNAL INFLUENCES

Here's a prayer for protection from external influences:

Heavenly Father,

I come before you seeking your divine protection for my marriage. In a world filled with distractions and temptations, I ask for your guidance to shield us from harmful external influences.

Protect us from the negative forces that seek to divide us and weaken our bond. Guard our hearts and minds against the pressures of society that may lead us astray from our commitment to each other.

Grant us discernment to recognize those influences that are not in alignment with your will for our marriage. Help us to remain steadfast in our love and devotion to one another, anchored in the values and principles that honor you.

Surround us with your angels of protection, Lord, and fortify our relationship with your strength and grace. May your presence be a constant reminder of our shared purpose and the sacredness of our union.

As we navigate the challenges of life together, may we always turn to you for guidance and support. Keep us united in heart and spirit, bound by the love that you have blessed us with. In your Holy Name, I pray, Amen.

PRAYER FOR UNITY AND COMMUNICATION IN MARRIAGE

Here's a prayer for unity and communication in marriage:

Heavenly Father,

I humbly come before you today, lifting my marriage to your loving care. You are the source of all unity and understanding, and I ask for your guidance in strengthening the bond between my partner and me.

Grant us the wisdom to communicate with love and respect, to listen with open hearts, and to speak with kindness and patience. Help us to set aside our desires and egos, and to prioritize the needs and feelings of one another.

Fill our hearts with empathy and compassion, Lord, so that we may truly understand each other's perspectives and experiences. May our communication be a reflection of your unconditional love and acceptance.

Bind us together with cords of unity that cannot be easily broken, Lord. Help us to work as a team, supporting and encouraging each other in all aspects of our lives.

In moments of disagreement or discord, remind us of the strength that comes from unity. Guide us to find common ground and solutions that honor both our needs and desires.

Praying Against Marriage Attacks

Lord, I pray for unity and harmony to reign in our marriage, drawing us closer to each other and you. May our relationship be a testament to your grace and faithfulness.

In your holy name, I pray, Amen.

PRAYER FOR HEALING FROM PAST WOUNDS AND TRAUMA

Here's a prayer for healing from past wounds and trauma in the context of marriage:

Heavenly Father,

I come before you today with a heavy heart, burdened by the pain of past wounds and traumas that have affected my marriage. You are the ultimate healer, and I ask for your divine touch to bring healing and restoration to my relationship/marriage.

Lord, you know the depths of our hearts and the scars that linger from past hurts. I pray for the courage to confront these wounds with honesty and vulnerability, both within myself and with my partner.

Grant us the strength to forgive those who have caused us pain, and to release the bitterness and resentment that have held us captive. Help us to extend grace to one another, recognizing that we are all imperfect beings in need of your mercy.

Heal the brokenness within our marriage, Lord, and mend the fractures that have strained our relationship. Replace our pain with your peace, our fear with your faith, and our sorrow with your joy.

Lord, I surrender our past hurts and traumas into your loving hands, trusting that you can turn our pain into purpose and our struggles into strength. May your healing presence be felt deeply within our hearts and our homes.

In your mercy and grace, we find hope for a brighter future together. Thank you, Lord, for your faithfulness and your steadfast love. In Jesus' name, I pray, Amen.

Praying Against Marriage Attacks

CHAPTER 6

SEEKING SUPPORT AND GUIDANCE

If you're seeking support and guidance in your marriage, it's essential to reach out to trusted individuals or resources that can assist. Here are some steps you can take:

1. **Counseling or Therapy:** Consider seeking the help of a licensed marriage counselor or therapist who can provide professional support and guidance. They can offer valuable insights, tools, and strategies to address your specific challenges and strengthen your relationship.

2. **Support Groups:** Look for support groups or community organizations that focus on marriage and relationships. Connecting with others who may be facing similar struggles can provide empathy, encouragement, and practical advice.

3. **Religious or Spiritual Guidance:** If you're part of a religious or spiritual community, consider seeking guidance from a trusted religious leader, such as a

pastor, priest, rabbi, or imam. They can offer spiritual counsel and support grounded in your faith tradition.

4.   Books and Resources: There are many books, articles, and online resources available that offer insights and practical tips for improving marriages. Look for reputable sources written by experts in the field of relationships and marriage.

5.   Communication with Your Partner: Open and honest communication with your partner is crucial. Express your feelings, concerns, and desires respectfully and constructively. Together, you can work as a team to identify areas of improvement and implement positive changes.

6.   Self-care: Take care of yourself physically, emotionally, and mentally. Practice self-care activities that help reduce stress and promote well-being, such as exercise, meditation, hobbies, and spending time with supportive friends and family members.

7.   Set Boundaries: Establish healthy boundaries within your marriage to protect your emotional and mental health. Communicate your needs and expectations to your partner, and respect their boundaries as well.

8. Patience and Perseverance: Remember that strengthening a marriage takes time, effort, and patience. Be willing to invest in the process of growth and improvement, and persevere through challenges together as a couple.

By seeking support and guidance from various sources, you can gain valuable insights and resources to help navigate the complexities of marriage and strengthen your relationship with your partner.

IMPORTANCE OF SEEKING COUNSELING AND COMMUNITY SUPPORT

Seeking counseling and community support can be incredibly beneficial for individuals and couples facing challenges in their relationships. Here are some reasons why it's important:

1. Professional Guidance: Marriage counselors and therapists are trained professionals with expertise in helping individuals and couples navigate relationship issues. They can provide valuable insights, tools, and strategies tailored to your specific needs and circumstances.

2. Objective Perspective: Counseling offers an objective perspective on your relationship dynamics.

A trained counselor can help you identify patterns of behavior, communication styles, and underlying issues that may be contributing to conflicts or challenges in your marriage.

3. Improved Communication Skills:

Counseling can help improve communication skills between partners. Learning how to express thoughts and feelings effectively, actively listen to each other, and resolve conflicts constructively are essential components of healthy relationships.

4. Validation and Support: Counseling provides a safe and supportive environment where you can express your concerns, fears, and vulnerabilities without judgment. Having a neutral third party validate your experiences and emotions can be validating and empowering.

5. Conflict Resolution: Counseling equips couples with tools and techniques for resolving conflicts and disagreements healthily and productively. Learning how to compromise, negotiate, and find common ground can strengthen the bond between partners.

6. Identifying Unhealthy Patterns:

Counseling can help identify unhealthy patterns or dynamics within the relationship, such as codependency, control issues, or unresolved trauma. Once these patterns are recognized, couples can work together to address them and create healthier dynamics.

7. Emotional Healing:
Counseling provides an opportunity for emotional healing and growth for both individuals and the relationship as a whole. Processing past wounds, traumas, and unresolved issues can lead to greater understanding, empathy, and connection between partners.

8. Preventive Maintenance:
Seeking counseling before significant problems arise can serve as preventive maintenance for your relationship. Regular check-ins with a counselor can help identify potential issues early on and address them proactively, reducing the likelihood of more significant problems down the road.

9. Community Support:
Engaging with a community of individuals or couples facing similar challenges can provide empathy, validation, and encouragement. Knowing that you're not alone in your struggles can offer a sense of solidarity and support as you work through your relationship issues.

10. Commitment to Growth: Seeking counseling and community support demonstrates a commitment to personal and relational growth. It shows that you're willing to invest time, effort, and resources into strengthening your relationship and building a healthier, more fulfilling partnership.

Overall, seeking counseling and community support can play a crucial role in helping individuals and couples navigate the complexities of relationships, overcome challenges, and build stronger, more resilient partnerships.

RESOURCES FOR FURTHER SPIRITUAL GROWTH AND STRENGTHENING MARRIAGE

Here are some resources for further spiritual growth and strengthening your marriage:

1. Individual and Couples Counseling:

Seek guidance from a trusted pastoral counselor or licensed therapist who integrates faith-based principles into their practice.

Consider attending marriage counseling or therapy sessions together to address specific challenges and strengthen your relationship.

Praying Against Marriage Attacks

2. Prayer and Meditation:

Set aside time for prayer and meditation individually and as a couple. Pray for guidance, wisdom, and strength in your marriage.

Incorporate spiritual practices such as mindfulness, gratitude, and reflection into your daily routine to deepen your spiritual connection with each other and with a higher power.

3. Community Support and Fellowship:

Engage with other couples within your faith community for support, encouragement, and accountability.

Join small groups, Bible studies, or marriage ministries offered by your church or religious organization to connect with like-minded couples on a deeper spiritual level.

4. Online Resources and Podcasts:

Explore online resources and podcasts focused on marriage and spirituality, such as Family Life Today, Marriage Today, or The Naked Marriage Podcast.

Follow blogs or websites that offer practical advice, insights, and inspiration for strengthening marriages from a spiritual perspective.

By engaging with these resources and incorporating spiritual principles into your marriage, you can deepen your connection with each other and with your faith, fostering growth, unity, and resilience in your relationship.

ENCOURAGEMENT AND HOPE FOR COUPLES FACING MARRIAGE ATTACKS

For couples facing marriage attacks, it's important to remember that challenges are a natural part of any relationship, and they can be overcome with patience, resilience, and support. Here's some encouragement and hope for couples navigating difficult times in their marriage:

1. You're Not Alone: Remember that you and your partner are in this together. Facing challenges as a team can strengthen your bond and resilience. Lean on each other for support and encouragement during tough times.

2. Growth Through Adversity: Difficulties in marriage can be opportunities for growth and learning. Embrace the challenges as a chance to deepen your understanding of each other and strengthen your relationship.

Praying Against Marriage Attacks

3.   Seek Help: Don't hesitate to seek professional help if needed. Marriage counseling or therapy can provide valuable guidance and support in navigating complex issues and finding solutions.

4.   Communication is Key: Keep the lines of communication open with your partner. Honest and respectful communication is essential for addressing problems, finding common ground, and rebuilding trust.

5.   Focus on Solutions: Instead of dwelling on the problems, focus on finding solutions together. Approach challenges with a mindset of collaboration and problem-solving rather than blame or defensiveness.

6.   Take Care of Yourselves: Remember to prioritize self-care for both yourself and your partner. Taking care of your physical, emotional, and mental wellbeing will help you better cope with stress and challenges in your marriage.

7.   Lean on Your Faith: If you have a spiritual or religious foundation, draw strength from your faith. Prayer, meditation, and seeking guidance from spiritual leaders can provide comfort and guidance during difficult times. **8. Celebrate Small Victories:** Acknowledge and celebrate the progress you make together, no matter how small. Every step forward is a testament to your commitment and resilience as a couple.

9.   Stay Committed: Remind yourselves of the love and commitment you share. Keep your focus on the long-term vision for your marriage and the life you're building together.

10.   Hope for the Future: Hold onto hope for the future. With determination, patience, and support, you can overcome the challenges you're facing and emerge stronger as individuals and as a couple.

Remember that every marriage faces its own unique set of challenges, and it's okay to ask for help and support along the way. Stay committed to each other and to the vision you have for your marriage, and trust that with time and effort, you can weather any storm together.

Praying Against Marriage Attacks

COMMITMENT TO CONTINUED PRAYER AND SPIRITUAL WARFARE IN MARRIAGE

Committing to continued prayer and spiritual warfare in marriage is a powerful decision that can deeply strengthen your relationship and fortify it against external attacks. Here are some thoughts on how to approach this commitment:

1.   Daily Prayer Together: Set aside time each day to pray together as a couple. This can be in the morning, before bed, or at any other convenient time. Pray for guidance, wisdom, and protection over your marriage, as well as for strength to face any challenges that may arise.

2.   Pray for Specific Needs: Be intentional about praying for specific needs and concerns within your marriage. This could include areas such as communication, trust, intimacy, and unity. Lift any struggles or conflicts you may be facing to God, asking for His intervention and guidance.

3.   Declare Scripture: Incorporate scripture into your prayers as a way to declare truth and spiritual protection over your marriage. Find verses that speak to the challenges you're facing and declare them together as a couple, believing in God's promises and provision.

4.   Engage in Spiritual Warfare: Recognize that marriage is not just a union between two individuals but also a spiritual bond. Engage in spiritual warfare by praying against any spiritual attacks or influences that may seek to harm your marriage. Use the authority given to you through Christ to rebuke any negative forces and claim victory in His name.

5.   Seek Spiritual Community: Surround yourselves with a supportive spiritual community that can provide encouragement, accountability, and prayer support. Consider joining a small group, attending couples' retreats or workshops, or connecting with other like-minded couples who are also committed to spiritual growth in their marriages.

6.   Stay Rooted in God's Word: Make reading and studying the Bible together a priority in your marriage. Allow God's Word to guide and shape your relationship, providing wisdom, insight, and encouragement as you navigate life's ups and downs together.

Praying Against Marriage Attacks

7. Practice Gratitude and Praise:

Cultivate an attitude of gratitude and praise in your marriage. Regularly thank God for the blessings He has given you, both individually and as a couple. Celebrate His faithfulness and goodness in your lives, even amidst challenges.

8. Stay Persistent and Consistent:

Recognize that spiritual warfare is an ongoing battle, and commitment to prayer and spiritual growth requires persistence and consistency. Even on days when you feel discouraged or distracted, make a conscious effort to prioritize prayer and spiritual connection in your marriage.

By committing to continued prayer and spiritual warfare in your marriage, you invite God into the center of your relationship, trusting in His power to strengthen, protect, and guide you both as you journey together in love and faith.

CONCLUSION

In conclusion, strengthening a marriage against attacks and fostering spiritual growth within the relationship requires intentional effort, commitment, and the utilization of various resources and strategies. By prioritizing open communication, trust, and mutual respect, couples can navigate challenges more effectively and deepen their bond over time. Seeking support from counselors, spiritual leaders, and community resources can provide valuable guidance and encouragement along the journey. Additionally, incorporating spiritual practices, such as prayer, meditation, and studying sacred texts, can nurture the spiritual connection within the marriage and help couples align their values and goals. Ultimately, by investing in the well-being of their relationship and drawing on both practical and spiritual resources, couples can cultivate a strong, resilient marriage that honors their commitment to each other and a higher purpose.

Praying Against Marriage Attacks

ABOUT THE AUTHOR

HART STEWART is a passionate advocate for spiritual empowerment and a dedicated practitioner of prayer warfare. With a deep-rooted belief in the power of faith and divine intervention, and has devoted her life to guiding individuals toward spiritual enlightenment and protection, particularly in the sacred institution of marriage.

Drawing from years of personal experience and spiritual insight, she has become a trusted voice in the realm of spiritual warfare, offering invaluable guidance and support to those facing challenges in their marital journey. Through their unwavering commitment to prayer and their profound understanding of spiritual principles, she has helped countless individuals overcome obstacles and strengthen their bonds with their partners.

As an author, speaker, and spiritual mentor, she brings a unique blend of wisdom, compassion, and unwavering faith to her work. Her mission is to empower individuals to stand firm against the forces that seek to undermine their marriages, equipping them with the tools and strategies needed to safeguard their relationships and cultivate lasting love and harmony.

With "Praying Against Marriage Attacks," HART STEWART offers a powerful resource for couples seeking divine protection and guidance in their marital journey. Through heartfelt prayers and spiritual insights, and provides a roadmap for couples to fortify their union and overcome any challenges they may face. This book is a testament to the Author's deep commitment to helping couples thrive in their marriages and experience the fullness of God's blessings in their lives.